Learn to Read Serbian in 5 Days

LENA DRAGOVIĆ

Copyright © 2018

Published by Wolfedale Press 2018

WOLFEDALE PRESS

All rights reserved. No part of this publication may be reproduced, distributed, or transmitted in any form or by any means, including photocopying, recording, or other electronic or mechanical methods, without the prior written permission of the publisher.

ISBN-13: 978-1-988800-04-2

CONTENTS

Introduction	i
Unit 1 – а, е, о, к, м, т	1
Unit 2 – р, с, в, j	3
Unit 3 – у, н, х, б	7
Unit 4 – л, п, д, з	9
Unit 5 – и, ч, ц, ж	11
Unit 6 – г, ш, ф	13
Unit 7 – ћ, џ, ђ	15
Unit 8 – љ, њ	17
Unit 9 – Review	19
Serbian Alphabet	21
Glossary – Thematic Order	23
Glossary – Alphabetical Order	31

INTRODUCTION

Learning a new alphabet can be very intimidating for an English speaker only used to reading the Latin alphabet. This is partly why English speakers tend to stick to learning other languages that use the same alphabet, such as French, Spanish and Italian – because they seem a lot easier!

But learning a new alphabet does not have to be so difficult. The difficulty is finding a good system to learn the new alphabet so that you don't get discouraged and give up before you make real progress. Making progress in the language is the best motivator.

The secret to learning a new alphabet is to be taught how to pronounce each letter separately, and then to practice how the new letters combine with letters you already know to read real words in the alphabet in a structured way. This is not revolutionary – it is most likely how you learned to read English – but it is not easy to find for other languages.

This book will teach you how to read the Serbian alphabet in exactly that way, and with this method you will be able to read Serbian in only 5 days or less! After that you will be able to enjoy the Serbian language and culture in a way that you were never able to before.

THE SERBIAN ALPHABET
српска ћирилица

The Serbian language uses 30 letters of the Cyrillic alphabet and is written from left to right. It uses the same basic letters as some other eastern Slavic languages, such as Russian and Bulgarian, as well as several non-Slavic languages from the former U.S.S.R. Although Serbian uses the same alphabet as Russian, there are differences in pronunciation between some of the letters in Serbian and Russian, just as there are differences in pronunciation between French, Spanish and English even though they use the same alphabet.

Although it is different from the Latin alphabet used to write English (and other European languages) the Serbian Cyrillic alphabet is not a difficult alphabet to learn to read. This is because, with almost no exceptions, letters are pronounced as they are written and written as they are pronounced in Serbian, unlike languages like English that make use of a lot of silent letters and historical spellings.

Like the Latin alphabet used to write English, the Serbian Cyrillic alphabet has both upper and lowercase letters. Upper case letters are used at the beginning of a sentence and in proper nouns. In Serbian most of the uppercase letters are the same shape as the lowercase letters, just larger.

Serbian speakers also use the Latin alphabet to write Serbian. This Latin alphabet is the same as the alphabet used to write the neighboring Croatian language. This book will use the Serbian/Croatian Latin alphabet in the pronunciation sections in order to not introduce a new Latin alphabet for the learner.

HOW TO USE THIS COURSE

The primary goal of this course book is to teach the reader to recognize the Serbian alphabet and to begin to read the Serbian language.

The main way this is accomplished is by teaching the individual pronunciations of each letter, and then utilizing "Practice" sections where the reader can practice reading real Serbian words. These "Practice" sections are very important and the main way the reader will start to feel comfortable with the Serbian alphabet. The answers to all "Practice" questions are included directly below the questions, but try to avoid looking at the answers until you have attempted to answer the questions yourself.

Throughout the book, the reader will also learn approximately 150 real Serbian words. These words have been carefully selected to be of maximum benefit to beginner students of the language and are a great starting point for students who want to continue their study of Serbian. In the end of the book there are two glossaries – one in thematic order and one in alphabetical order – where the student can study and memorize all the words learned in this course.

The course material has been designed to be completed slowly over 5 days, while reviewing lessons as necessary. You are encouraged to go at whatever pace you feel comfortable with and to feel free to go back to lessons to review as much as needed.

Good luck and I hope you enjoy the first step on your journey to learning the Serbian language.

UNIT 1 - а, е, о, к, м, т

The first 6 letters introduced in this course are the letters in Serbian that resemble English letters and are pronounced roughly the same. Basically, you already know these six Serbian letters!

The letter а in Serbian is pronounced like the "a" sound in the English words "spa" or "father" (IPA: /ɑ/). The uppercase form is А.

The letter е is pronounced like the "e" sound in the English words "met" or "peg" (IPA: /ɛ/). The uppercase form is Е.

The letter о is pronounced like the "o" sound in the English word "not" or "octopus" (IPA: /ɔ/). The uppercase form is О.

The letter к is pronounced like the "k" sound in the English words "kick" or "kite" (IPA: /k/). The uppercase form is К.

The letter м is pronounced like the "m" sound in the English words "mother" or "Michael" (IPA: /m/). The uppercase form is М.

The letter т is pronounced like the "t" sound in the English words "tan" or "Tom" (IPA: /t/). The uppercase form is Т.

As you can see these 6 letters are virtually the same as in English!

PRACTICE

Try to recognize these English words in their Serbian disguises. The answers are below.

1. ат
2. мет
3. кат
4. так
5. кот
6. мат
7. мама

ANSWERS

1. at
2. met
3. cat
4. tack
5. cot
6. mat
7. mama

UNIT 2 - p, c, в, j

The four letters introduced in this unit look like letters you already know, but unlike Unit 1 these letters are not pronounced the same as in English. Pay close attention to these letters and avoid pronouncing them like in English.

The letter **p** is pronounced like the Spanish "r" sound in "rapido", i.e. a trilled or rolled "r" sound (IPA: /r/). This letter is not difficult to pronounce for an English speaker but does require some practice. If you cannot pronounce this letter yet, you can substitute an English "r" sound for now. Although this letter resembles an English "p" it is not pronounced like a "p" sound. The uppercase form is **P**.

The letter **c** is pronounced like the "s" sound in "some" or "same" (IPA: /s/). Although it resembles an English "c", it is never pronounced like the "c" in "cat". It is always pronounced with an "s" sound. The hard "c" sound is spelled with к in Serbian. The uppercase form is C.

The letter **в** is pronounced like the "v" sound in "very" (IPA: /v/). Although it resembles an uppercase "B", it is never pronounced like the English "b" sound in "boy". The uppercase form is **B**.

The letter **j** is pronounced like the "y" in "yes", or the "y" in "boy" (IPA: /j/). The uppercase form is J. Although this letter is never pronounced like the English "j" sound in "jump", the Serbian Latin alphabet uses the letter "j" to represent the "y" sound and this convention will be followed throughout this course.

PRACTICE 1

Try to recognize these English words in their Serbian disguises. Focus on the correct pronunciation and not necessarily the English spelling. The answers are below.

1. рат
2. тoj
3. jес
4. вет
5. матс
6. котс
7. рот
8. мор
9. стем
10. сторм

ANSWERS 1

1. rat
2. toy
3. yes
4. vet
5. mats
6. cots
7. rot
8. more
9. stem
10. storm

PRACTICE 2

Try to read these real Serbian words. The English translation is given next to each word. The correct pronunciations are given in the answers below.

1. мај   (May)
2. море   (sea)
3. тата   (daddy / papa)
4. сестра   (sister)
5. сто   (table)
6. врата   (door)
7. крв   (blood)
8. кост   (bone)

ANSWERS 2

1. maj (pronounced like "my")
2. more
3. tata
4. sestra
5. sto
6. vrata
7. krv
8. kost

UNIT 3 - у, н, х, б

The Serbian letter у is pronounced like the "oo" sound in "boot" or the end of the word "shoe" (IPA: /u/). Although this letter resembles an English "y", it is not pronounced like the "y" sound in "yesterday" or the "y" sound in "tiny". This letter will be represented as "u" in this book. The uppercase form is У.

The Serbian letter н is pronounced like the "n" sound in "now" or "hen" (IPA: /n/). Pay close attention to this letter as it resembles an uppercase "H" in English, but should not be pronounced like an "h" sound. The uppercase form is Н.

The pronunciation of the Serbian letter х does not exist in English. It is the "ch" sound in the German "doch" or the "j" sound in the Spanish "ojos" (IPA: /x/). It is a heavy throat clearing "h" sound. This letter will be represented by "h" in this book to match the Serbian Latin spelling. The uppercase form is Х.

The letter б is pronounced like the "b" sound in "best" (IPA: /b/). Pay close attention to the letters б and в. The letter б, which looks like the number "6", is pronounced "b" and the letter в, which looks like an uppercase "B", is pronounced "v". With some practice this will become easier. The uppercase form is Б.

PITCH ACCENT IN SERBIAN

Serbian is often described as a tonal or pitch accented language, as the pitch and contour of a vowel can affect the meaning of the word, especially for minimal pairs that would otherwise be pronounced identically.

In Serbian-English dictionaries you will often see an accent written on the vowel to describe the tonal pitch of a Serbian word. These accents, however, are not normally written in the language and therefore will not be included in the Serbian words in this book.

PRACTICE

Try to read these real Serbian words. The English translation is given next to each word. The correct pronunciations are given in the answers below.

1. ауто (car)
2. уста (mouth)
3. банка (bank)
4. нос (nose)
5. храна (food)
6. боја (color)
7. бео (white)
8. небо (sky)
9. сутра (tomorrow)

ANSWERS

1. auto
2. usta
3. banka
4. nos
5. hrana
6. boja
7. beo
8. nebo
9. sutra

UNIT 4 - л, п, д, з

The Serbian letter л is pronounced like the "l" sound in "little" or "like" (IPA: /l/). The uppercase form is Л.

The letter п is pronounced like the "p" sound in "pie" or "pepper" (IPA: /p/). The Serbian letter resembles the Greek letter pi that you probably remember from geometry. This is not a coincidence as the Cyrillic alphabet derives from the Greek alphabet and some letters look very similar. The uppercase form is П.

The letter д is pronounced like the "d" sound in "dad" (IPA: /d/). The uppercase form is Д.

The letter з is pronounced like the "z" in "zoo" or "zebra" (IPA: /z/). The uppercase form is З.

PRACTICE

Try to read these Serbian words. The English translation is given next to each word. The correct pronunciations are given in the answers below.

1. хотел   (hotel)
2. тело   (body)
3. стопало   (foot)
4. хлеб   (bread)
5. плав   (blue)
6. зелен   (green)
7. лед   (ice)
8. хладан   (cold)

9. дрво   (tree)
10. добар   (good)
11. један   (one)
12. пазар   (market)

ANSWERS

1. hotel
2. telo
3. stopalo
4. hleb
5. plav
6. zelen
7. led
8. hladan
9. drvo
10. dobar
11. jedan
12. pazar

UNIT 5 - и, ч, ц, ж

The Serbian letter и, which looks like an uppercase "N" written backwards, is pronounced like the "i" sound in "machine" or the "ee" sound in "bee" (IPA: /i/). This letter is spelled "i" in Serbian Latin. The uppercase form is И.

The letter ч is pronounced like the "ch" sound in "church" (IPA: /tʃ/). Although written with two letters in English, it is really a single sound and is only written with one letter in Serbian. This letter will be represented in this book by č. The uppercase form is Ч.

The letter ц is pronounced like the "ts" sound in "cats" (IPA: /ts/). This is really two sounds, a "t" sound followed by an "s" sound, but it is written with only one letter in Serbian. In the Serbian Latin alphabet, this letter is written with a "c". This can be a little confusing as it does not match the English pronunciation of "c", however this convention has been used in this book in order to help the reader become acquainted with this common usage. Remember when you see a "c" in the pronunciation sections that it is pronounced "ts". Unlike English, in Serbian this letter can be used at the beginning of a word and is still pronounced "ts". The uppercase form is Ц.

The letter ж is pronounced like the "s" sound in "pleasure" or "measure" (IPA: /ʒ/). This letter will be represented in this book as ž. The uppercase form is Ж.

PRACTICE

Try to read these Serbian words. The English translation is given next to each word. The correct pronunciations are given in the answers below.

1. улица   (street)
2. авион   (airplane)
3. риба   (fish)
4. човек   (man)
5. дечак   (boy)
6. чамац   (boat)
7. жут   (yellow)
8. тужан   (sad)
9. месец   (month)
10. птица   (bird)

ANSWERS

1. ulica (pronounced "ulitsa")
2. avion
3. riba
4. čovek
5. dečak
6. čamac
7. žut
8. tužan
9. mesec
10. ptica

UNIT 6 - г, ш, ф

The letter г is pronounced like the "g" sound in "good", (IPA: /g/). The uppercase form is Г.

The letter ш is pronounced like the "sh" sound in "short" (IPA: /ʃ/). Although written with two letters in English, it is really one sound and it is written with one letter in Serbian. This letter will be represented in this book by š. The uppercase form is Ш.

The letter ф is pronounced like the "f" sound in "food" (IPA: /f/). The uppercase form is Ф.

PRACTICE

Try to read these Serbian words. The English translation is given next to each word. The correct pronunciations are given in the answers below.

1. град   (city)
2. глава   (head)
3. нога   (leg)
4. снег   (snow)
5. киша   (rain)
6. лош   (bad)
7. шест   (six)
8. миш   (mouse)
9. школа   (school)
10. кафа   (coffee)
11. јефтин   (cheap)
12. фебруар   (February)

ANSWERS

1. grad
2. glava
3. noga
4. sneg
5. kiša
6. loš
7. šest
8. miš
9. škola
10. kafa
11. jeftin
12. februar

UNIT 7 - ћ, џ, ђ

✳ The letter ћ is pronounced like the "ch" sound in "ching" (IPA: /tɕ/). This letter is written ć in Serbian Latin. ћ is pronounced very similarly to ч, and the two sounds are difficult to tell apart, even for many native speakers. Technically, however, the "ch" sound in ћ is a little softer than the "ch" sound in ч. The uppercase form is Ћ.

The letter џ is pronounced like the "dg" sound in "dodge" (IPA: /dʒ/). This letter is written dž in Serbian Latin. The uppercase form is Џ.

✳ The letter ђ is pronounced like the "j" sound in "Jack". (IPA: /dʑ/). This letter is written đ in Serbian Latin. The pronunciation of ђ and џ are very similar, with ђ being pronounced a little softer than џ. The sounds of these letters are difficult to distinguish for English speakers, but you will be understood as a beginner if you use an English "j" sound for both. The uppercase form is Ђ. Notice that this letter is very similar looking to h but is pronounced differently.

PRACTICE

Try to read these Serbian words. The English translation is given next to each word. The correct pronunciations are given in the answers below.

1. врућ   (hot)
2. срећан   (happy)
3. кћи   (daughter)
4. кућа   (house)
5. дућан   (store / shop)
6. одећа   (clothing)

7. ђак   (pupil / student)
8. џак   (sack / bag)
9. леђа   (back)
10. џем   (jam)

ANSWERS

1. vruć
2. srećan
3. kći
4. kuća
5. dućan
6. odeća
7. đak
8. džak
9. leđa
10. džem

UNIT 8 - љ, њ

The letter љ looks like the letter л but with a small "b" attached to it. This letter is pronounced like the "lli" sound in "million". (IPA: /ʎ/). This letter is written as lj in Serbian Latin, and that is the convention that will be used in this course. The uppercase form is Љ.

The letter њ looks like the letter н but with a small "b" attached to it. It is pronounced like the "ny" sound in "canyon" (IPA: /ɲ/). This letter is written as nj in Serbian Latin, and that is the convention that will be used in this course. The uppercase form is Њ.

PRACTICE

Try to read these Serbian words. The English translation is given next to each word. The correct pronunciations are given in the answers below.

1. земља   (country)
2. хаљина   (dress)
3. кошуља   (shirt)
4. коњ   (horse)
5. свиња   (pig)
6. књига   (book)

ANSWERS

1. zemlja (pronounced "zemlya")
2. haljina
3. košulja
4. konj
5. svinja
6. knjiga

UNIT 9 - REVIEW

PRACTICE 1

Review the previous lessons by reading these real Serbian place names below. The correct pronunciations are given in the answers below.
1. Србија
2. Београд
3. Нови Сад
4. Крагујевац
5. Дунав
6. Тамиш
7. Бабичка Гора
8. Бањско Брдо

ANSWERS 1

1. Srbija (Serbia)
2. Beograd (Belgrade)
3. Novi Sad
4. Kragujevac
5. Dunab (Danube)
6. Tamiš
7. Babička Gora
8. Banjsko Brdo

PRACTICE 2

Review what you have learned in this book by reading the Serbian names below. The correct pronunciations are given in the answers below.
1. Вучић
2. Брнабић
3. Николић
4. Ђорђевић
5. Гашић
6. Анђелић
7. Вукобратовић
8. Ајдачић

ANSWERS 2

1. Vučić
2. Brnabić
3. Nikolić
4. Đorđević
5. Gašić
6. Anđelić
7. Vukobratović
8. Ajdačić

SERBIAN ALPHABET

Cyrillic	Roman	Pronunciation
А а	A a	[a]
Б б	B b	[b]
В в	V v	[v]
Г г	G g	[g]
Д д	D d	[d]
Ђ ђ	Đ đ	[dʑ]
Е е	E e	[e]
Ж ж	Ž ž	[ʒ]
З з	Z z	[z]
И и	I i	[i]
Ј ј	J j	[j]
К к	K k	[k]
Л л	L l	[l]
Љ љ	Lj lj	[ʎ]
М м	M m	[m]

Н н	N n	[n]
Њ њ	Nj nj	[ɲ]
О о	O o	[o]
П п	P p	[p]
Р р	R r	[ɾ]
С с	S s	[s]
Т т	T t	[t]
Ћ ћ	Ć ć	[tɕ]
У у	U u	[u]
Ф ф	F f	[f]
Х х	H h	[x]
Ц ц	C c	[ts]
Ч ч	Č č	[tʂ]
Џ џ	Dž dž	[dʐ]
Ш ш	Š š	[ʂ]

GLOSSARY – THEMATIC ORDER

ANIMALS

животиња	[životinja]	animal
пас	[pas]	dog
мачка	[mačka]	cat
риба	[riba]	fish
птица	[ptica]	bird
крава	[krava]	cow
свиња	[svinja]	pig
миш	[miš]	mouse
коњ	[konj]	horse

PEOPLE

особа	[osoba]	person
мајка	[majka]	mother
мама	[mama]	mommy / mama
отац	[otac]	father
тата	[tata]	daddy / papa
син	[sin]	son
кћи	[kći]	daughter
брат	[brat]	brother
сестра	[sestra]	sister
пријатељ	[prijatelj]	friend
човек	[čovek]	man
жена	[žena]	woman
дечак	[dečak]	boy
девојка	[devojka]	girl
дете	[dete]	child

TRANSPORTATION

воз	[voz]	train
авион	[avion]	airplane
ауто	[auto]	car (automobile)
бицикл	[bicikl]	bicycle
аутобус	[autobus]	bus
чамац	[čamac]	boat

LOCATION

град	[grad]	city
кућа	[kuća]	house
улица	[ulica]	street
аеродром	[aerodrom]	airport
хотел	[hotel]	hotel
ресторан	[restoran]	restaurant
школа	[škola]	school
универзитет	[univerzitet]	university
парк	[park]	park
дућан	[dućan]	store / shop
болница	[bolnica]	hospital
црква	[crkva]	church
земља	[zemlja]	country (state)
банка	[banka]	bank
пазар	[pazar]	market

HOME

сто	[sto]	table
столица	[stolica]	chair
прозор	[prozor]	window
врата	[vrata]	door
књига	[knjiga]	book

CLOTHING

одећа	[odeća]	clothing
шешир	[šešir]	hat
хаљина	[haljina]	dress
кошуља	[košulja]	shirt
панталоне	[pantalone]	pants
ципела	[cipela]	shoe

BODY

тело	[telo]	body
глава	[glava]	head
лице	[lice]	face
коса	[kosa]	hair
око	[oko]	eye
уста	[usta]	mouth
нос	[nos]	nose
уво	[uho]	ear
рука	[ruka]	hand / arm
стопало	[stopalo]	foot
нога	[noga]	leg
леђа	[leđa]	back
срце	[srce]	heart

крв	[krv]	blood
кост	[kost]	bone
брада	[brada]	beard

MISCELLANEOUS

| да | [da] | yes |
| не | [ne] | no |

FOOD & DRINK

храна	[hrana]	food
месо	[meso]	meat
хлеб	[hleb]	bread
сир	[sir]	cheese
јабука	[jabuka]	apple
вода	[voda]	water
пиво	[pivo]	beer
вино	[vino]	wine
кафа	[kafa]	coffee
чај	[čaj]	tea
млеко	[mleko]	milk
сок	[sok]	juice
доручак	[doručak]	breakfast
ручак	[ručak]	lunch
вечера	[večera]	dinner

COLORS

| боја | [boja] | color |
| црвен | [crven] | red |

плав	[plav]	blue
зелен	[zelen]	green
жут	[žut]	yellow
црн	[crn]	black
бео	[beo]	white

NATURE

море	[more]	sea
река	[reka]	river
језеро	[jezero]	lake
планина	[planina]	mountain
киша	[kiša]	rain
снег	[sneg]	snow
дрво	[drvo]	tree
цвет	[cvet]	flower
сунце	[sunce]	sun
месец	[mjesec]	moon
ветар	[vetar]	wind
небо	[nebo]	sky
ватра	[vatra]	fire
лед	[led]	ice

ADJECTIVES

велик	[velik]	big
мал	[mal]	small
добар	[dobar]	good
лош	[loš]	bad
врућ	[vruć]	hot
хладан	[hladan]	cold
јефтин	[jeftin]	cheap

скуп	[skup]	expensive
срећан	[srećan]	happy
тужан	[tužan]	sad

NUMBERS

један	[jedan]	one
два	[dva]	two
три	[tri]	three
четири	[četiri]	four
пет	[pet]	five
шест	[šest]	six
седам	[sedam]	seven
осам	[osam]	eight
девет	[devet]	nine
десет	[deset]	ten

TIME

дан	[dan]	day
месец	[mjesec]	month
година	[godina]	year
сат	[sat]	hour
данас	[danas]	today
сутра	[sutra]	tomorrow
јуче	[juče]	yesterday

DAYS OF THE WEEK

недеља	[nedelja]	Sunday
понедељак	[ponedeljak]	Monday
уторак	[utorak]	Tuesday
среда	[sreda]	Wednesday
четвртак	[četvrtak]	Thursday
петак	[petak]	Friday
субота	[subota]	Saturday

MONTHS

јануар	[januar]	January
фебруар	[februar]	February
март	[mart]	March
април	[april]	April
мај	[maj]	May
јун	[jun]	June
јул	[jul]	July
август	[avgust]	August
септембар	[septembar]	September
октобар	[oktobar]	October
новембар	[novembar]	November
децембар	[decembar]	December

PROPER NAMES

Србија	[srbija]	Serbia
Београд	[beograd]	Belgrade
Србин	[srbin]	Serb (person)
српски	[srpski]	Serbian (language)

GLOSSARY – ALPHABETICAL ORDER

– A a –

август	[avgust]	August
авион	[avion]	airplane
аеродром	[aerodrom]	airport
април	[april]	April
ауто	[auto]	car (automobile)
аутобус	[autobus]	bus

– Б б –

банка	[banka]	bank
бео	[beo]	white
Београд	[Beograd]	Belgrade
бицикл	[bicikl]	bicycle
боја	[boja]	color
болница	[bolnica]	hospital
брада	[brada]	beard
брат	[brat]	brother

– В в –

ватра	[vatra]	fire
велик	[velik]	big
ветар	[vetar]	wind
вечера	[večera]	dinner
вино	[vino]	wine
вода	[voda]	water
воз	[voz]	train

| врата | [vrata] | door |
| врућ | [vruć] | hot |

– Г г –

глава	[glava]	head
година	[godina]	year
град	[grad]	city

– Д д –

да	[da]	yes
дан	[dan]	day
данас	[danas]	today
два	[dva]	two
девет	[devet]	nine
девојка	[devojka]	girl
десет	[deset]	ten
дете	[dete]	child
децембар	[decembar]	December
дечак	[dečak]	boy
добар	[dobar]	good
доручак	[doručak]	breakfast
дрво	[drvo]	tree
дућан	[dućan]	store / shop

– Ж ж –

жена	[žena]	woman
животиња	[životinja]	animal
жут	[žut]	yellow

– З з –

зелен	[zelen]	green
земља	[zemlja]	country (state)

– J j –

јабука	[jabuka]	apple
јануар	[januar]	January
један	[jedan]	one
језеро	[jezero]	lake
јефтин	[jeftin]	cheap
јул	[jul]	July
јун	[jun]	June
јуче	[juče]	yesterday

– К к –

кафа	[kafa]	coffee
киша	[kiša]	rain
књига	[knjiga]	book
коњ	[konj]	horse
коса	[kosa]	hair
кост	[kost]	bone
кошуља	[košulja]	shirt
крава	[krava]	cow
крв	[krv]	blood
кћи	[kći]	daughter
кућа	[kuća]	house

– Л л –

лед	[led]	ice
леђа	[leđa]	back (body)
лице	[lice]	face
лош	[loš]	bad

– М м –

мај	[maj]	May
мајка	[majka]	mother
мал	[mal]	small
мама	[mama]	mommy / mama
март	[mart]	March
мачка	[mačka]	cat
месец	[mesec]	moon / month
месо	[meso]	meat
миш	[miš]	mouse
млеко	[mleko]	milk
море	[more]	sea

– Н н –

не	[ne]	no
небо	[nebo]	sky
недеља	[nedelja]	Sunday
новембар	[novembar]	November
нога	[noga]	leg
нос	[nos]	nose

– O o –

одећа	[odeća]	clothing
око	[oko]	eye
октобар	[oktobar]	October
осам	[osam]	eight
особа	[osoba]	person
отац	[otac]	father

– П п –

пазар	[pazar]	market
панталоне	[pantalone]	pants
парк	[park]	park
пас	[pas]	dog
пет	[pet]	five
петак	[petak]	Friday
пиво	[pivo]	beer
плав	[plav]	blue
планина	[planina]	mountain
понедељак	[ponedeljak]	Monday
пријатељ	[prijatelj]	friend
прозор	[prozor]	window
птица	[ptica]	bird

– Р р –

река	[reka]	river
ресторан	[restoran]	restaurant
риба	[riba]	fish
рука	[ruka]	hand / arm
ручак	[ručak]	lunch

– С с –

сат	[sat]	hour
свиња	[svinja]	pig
седам	[sedam]	seven
септембар	[septembar]	September
сестра	[sestra]	sister
син	[sin]	son
сир	[sir]	cheese
скуп	[skup]	expensive
снег	[sneg]	snow
сок	[sok]	juice
Србија	[srbija]	Serbia
Србин	[srbin]	Serb (person)
среда	[sreda]	Wednesday
срећан	[srećan]	happy
српски	[srpski]	Serbian (lang.)
срце	[srce]	heart
сто	[sto]	table
столица	[stolica]	chair
стопало	[stopalo]	foot
субота	[subota]	Saturday
сунце	[sunce]	sun
сутра	[sutra]	tomorrow

– Т т –

тата	[tata]	daddy / papa
тело	[telo]	body
три	[tri]	three
тужан	[tužan]	sad

– У у –

уво	[uho]	ear
улица	[ulica]	street
универзитет	[univerzitet]	university
уста	[usta]	mouth
уторак	[utorak]	Tuesday

– Ф ф –

фебруар	[februar]	February

– Х х –

хаљина	[haljina]	dress
хладан	[hladan]	cold
хлеб	[hleb]	bread
хотел	[hotel]	hotel
храна	[hrana]	food

– Ц ц –

цвет	[cvet]	flower
ципела	[cipela]	shoe
црвен	[crven]	red
црква	[crkva]	church
црн	[crn]	black

– Ч ч –

чај	[čaj]	tea
чамац	[čamac]	boat
четвртак	[četvrtak]	Thursday
четири	[četiri]	four
човек	[čovek]	man

– Ш ш –

шест	[šest]	six
шешир	[šešir]	hat
школа	[škola]	school

Other language learning titles available from Wolfedale Press:

Learn to Read Arabic in 5 Days
Learn to Read Armenian in 5 Days
Learn to Read Bulgarian in 5 Days
Learn to Read Georgian in 5 Days
Learn to Read Greek in 5 Days
Learn to Read Modern Hebrew in 5 Days
Learn to Read Persian (Farsi) in 5 Days
Learn to Read Russian in 5 Days
Learn to Read Ukrainian in 5 Days